(fear not)

(fear not) Venture to inner peace

© Copyright 2005
Three Spirits Press, LLC

ISBN: 0-9760304-0-3
Library of Congress Card Number: 2004096459

Written by Alan Lohner
Photography: Jason Savage – all images except pages 23, 27 & 49
Photography: Cory Raff – pages 23, 27 & 49
Design: Cory Raff

Visit our website at www.ThreeSpiritsPress.com
for more information on (fear not) and other
books of higher purpose.

Printed in Canada

Dedicated to peace for men, women and children everywhere.

Seek the shelter within.

Only by searching inside ourselves can we find truth
and realize freedom from fear. The journey to inner peace
is not a simple one, but it is the sure path to happiness,
fulfillment and contentment. Easing that journey —
and helping you live with greater purpose —
is the reason for this book.

You can
change the past.

Dwell on the positive as you contemplate the past.
Anything you perceive as hurtful can be altered. By shifting
your thinking to the positive — no matter how challenging
this is — you put in motion real and effective change.

Welcome disappointments willingly.

When any expectation does not come to pass, accept it. Try to find a helpful lesson from the experience. Take what you learn to embrace new opportunities.

When you're hurting, help someone.

If things go wrong, a natural inclination is
to withdraw. Instead, reach beyond your pain and touch
the life of another in a positive way. By healing another,
you heal yourself.

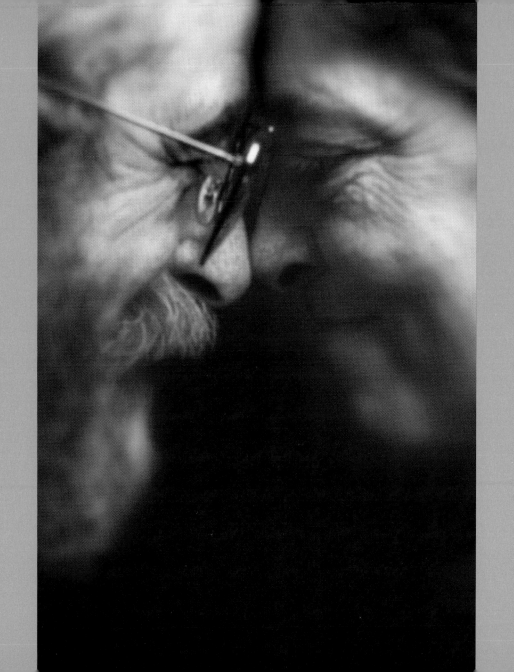

In giving is receiving.

If you perceive lack in your life, you are more
than likely giving less than you are able. It is totally
acceptable to desire more. To receive more,
learn to give more.

Love those
who leave you.

When you practice unconditional love, you align with
higher principles and open your heart to new possibilities.
Cast loving thoughts toward others, especially those who
have erred against you. Love is always a choice you can
make, and it is always the correct choice, even when
it is difficult to do so.

Failure is
all in your mind.

Why put a negative value on any outcome?

This limits your progress. Learning is present in any

endeavor, and this carries you forward.

Grace yourself with gratitude.

Make time every day to appreciate the good
things in your life, and you will see them multiply.
Give thanks for everything you have, and generously
give praise to others. Take not a single breath
for granted.

Small acts are
most important.

Everything you do creates a chain reaction.
You cannot see the ultimate outcome generated
by your deeds. The smallest kindness can be
a catalyst for the greatest good.

Suicide cannot end life.

It is not uncommon to flirt with suicidal thoughts
in times of crisis. But remember, there is no escape from
learning, and suicide creates more challenging lessons
in the next life. If someone you know has committed
suicide, send loving and compassionate thoughts to that
person, and this will bring comfort to both of you.

All mistakes
are correctable.

At first glance, this seems impossible.
However, you can correct any mistake simply by
changing the way you think about it. In this way,
you alone can right every wrong.

You were never born.

Your spiritual essence has no beginning and
no end. Knowing this brings joy and peace of mind.
And it enables you to more freely celebrate your
human side.

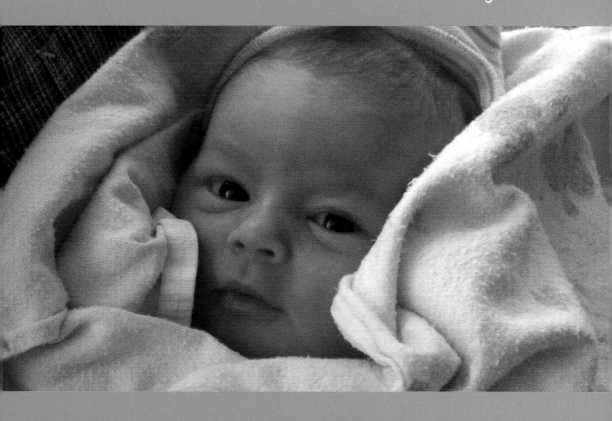

Death is an illusion.

Only your body will die. Your thoughts will continue on. Enjoy the physical realm you now inhabit, but do not attach too strongly to it, because your destiny is to transcend it.

Asking for help
is a strength.

If pride prevents you from seeking assistance,
that is a weakness. Turn your situation around.
Ask yourself, "Why deny another the gift
of helping me?"

There's an eternity
in every now.

Take memory snapshots in your mind throughout
your day. Review them often. Make it a point to appreciate
sunsets, flowers and children's laughter.

(fear not)

It's human to be fearful. But as you raise your
level of spiritual awareness, your fears will lessen. At the
highest state of awareness — which is our true and natural
condition — only love exists, where fear
cannot abide.

Enjoy abundance by giving freely.

Align yourself with a group, organization
or affiliation that is committed to good works.
Donate your time, talent or money to create a steady
flow of positive energy. See yourself as an active
participant in helping and healing others,
enhancing your self-image and further enabling
you to perpetuate goodness.

Expect miracles.

When you become absolutely clear on
an intention, it manifests. Keep in mind, however,
that miracles are not magical — they are a natural
outcome of supreme clarity. The moment that
uncertainty creeps into your thoughts,
miracles are put on hold.

Any assault—
verbal or physical—is an
appeal for help.

If you doubt this, you are not perceiving

it correctly. This is not to deny the pain and

anguish you may experience at the hands of another.

However, if you understand that all attack springs

from fear, you can more readily start the

healing process.

Learn to unlearn.

Incorrect beliefs can keep you from your dreams.
Recognize repeat patterns that reinforce self-doubt,
self-denial and self-depreciation. Reach out and ask
for help in breaking free from these cycles.

Unkindness
can be undone.

It is never too late to be kind. If you have erred against another, make restitution. By doing so, you give yourself a gift of reconciliation, which will empower you to be kinder to yourself.

Where there is fear, truth cannot be learned.

If something troubles you, face up to
it now. Avoiding a problem prolongs insecurity and
uncertainty. Suspend your fear and a resolution
will surface.

Love is never lost.

The love you gave — the love you give —
continues on and on. Learn to extend your heart
freely, without expectation, and you cannot lose, even if
you are rebuffed or ignored. Chase away negative
thoughts because these can bring you pain.

Listen loudly
to yourself.

When you feel a nudge, pay attention.
Trust your intuition, even if it flies in the face
of convention. Heed your dreams, hold your vision,
and drown out discouraging words with your
own inner voice.

Children
are our teachers.

Young people inhabit the same physical plane as
grown-ups, but reflect on how differently they live.
Listen to children and imitate the way they view
the world. We can unlearn fear and prejudice
by a child's example.

You know your reason for being.

Your higher self understands why you are here.
Bringing this awareness to your conscious mind is
both your greatest blessing and greatest challenge.
Quiet contemplation is your pathway
to discovery.

In anything that befalls you, find the gift in it.

Whatever happens in your life, if you look for a positive circumstance, you will find it. This is a most challenging truth. When you uncover the gift in a hard situation, it enables you to grow stronger in mind and spirit.

Create good thoughts.

Positive thinking generates positive energy.

You alone determine your happiness and well-being.

Expect good things to happen.

Accept responsibility for everything in your life.

Even if life seems unfair, even if you feel victimized in some way, change your thoughts about this. Consider the possibility that you chose your path and purpose. The more challenging your path, the greater the opportunity for spiritual advancement.

Children who pass away are the greatest teachers of all.

In a world filled with fear and guilt, children who depart the physical plane leave a legacy of love and innocence. Emulate these master teachers and know that they are with you always. Respect their memory by leading an honorable life.

(fear not)

If you choose, everything that happens in your life
can be viewed as experience. Look around you and place
no judgment on anything you see. The world is,
and nothing more.

The less you own,
the freer you are.

If you attach to the material world too strongly,

it's more difficult to be in touch with your spiritual side.

Enjoy your possessions but know that they carry a price.

Live as simply as you can, as comfortably as you need.

You are safe
within yourself.

A still mind has no limits in space or time.
Learn to find this place of inner solitude. Be prepared
for important insights to come to you in
the quiet.

Love yourself first.

On the face of it, this sounds selfish. But how
can you extend love to another, if love isn't strong
within you? Affirm your goodness every
moment of your life.

Take nothing personally.

No matter how personal something feels,
it isn't. Resist negative feelings about another's actions.
Remember that people act out of issues that cloud
their reality, not yours.

Set the world free.

See yourself as a helper for anyone who crosses your path. Harbor no grievances toward another, because this has a boomerang effect. How you treat others is ultimately how you treat yourself.

Nothing is as ugly as you imagine.

Everything is as it is. Therefore, see the beauty and the bounty in all things. As you improve this ability, you'll become more in tune to the world around you, and in turn, you'll attract greater goodness to your life.

In the absence
of love, love.

How difficult it is to extend loving thoughts
when another disappoints us. Reject anger, jealousy
and vengeance. These perpetuate hurt
and suffering.

We live in
our thoughts.

One day your body will cease to be. Prepare for
that certainty now. If you fill your mind with higher
truths, you will more easily make the transition
to full spiritual life.

Beware the weight of words.

Choose and use words with care. Never underestimate the power of encouraging comments, compassionate dialogue, or even simple conversation. The written word is no less powerful.

Peace cannot be won—it can only be accepted.

The more you struggle for peace, the more it eludes you. Learn to let go. Peace is always at hand should you simply choose it.

See with a child's eyes.

Carefree and innocent, children are the embodiment
on earth of all that is divine. Strip away all that you know
about something, and look at it as if for the very first time.
Extend this exercise to as much as you can as often
as you can.

Forgive and find peace.

From your spiritual side, it is simple.

From your human side, it is difficult. Which side

will you honor more?

Show your true face.

What part of you insists on hiding behind a mask?
When you can answer that question, you unlock the
potential for great personal understanding and growth.
Be real and attain what you really want.

Laugh like a baby.

Humor yourself and those around you.
Laughter, like love, is contagious. Use it in
large measure.

(fear not)

Two negative words are transformed into a single
positive affirmation. What negative thoughts can you
transform? Redirect one negative thought right
now to show yourself that it can be done.

Waste makes worse.

Time, opportunities, money, food—what things
have you wasted in your life? It is self-destructive to
feel guilty, because this only leads to more waste.
Instead, focus on using resources wisely
from now on.

Take a hike.

Exercise stimulates the heart, mind and spirit.
Walk in the woods, on a beach, or anywhere outdoors,
and make it part of your regular routine. You will find
a healing energy in nature.

There's no such thing as too much love.

You can spoil someone with material things, but you cannot love too lavishly. Fear can restrict the capacity of your heart. Better to love freely now and never regret not loving enough.

Seek inner beauty.

You may revel in finding fault with another,
but this leads to separation and loss. Try to find
humanity in everyone you encounter. By overlooking
flaws in other people, you empower yourself to forgive
your own flaws, which hold you back.

Connect with everything.

Do all you can to reach out to people and places
you don't know. Immerse yourself in a new hobby or
pastime. Explore your community, your country,
your world.

Your mission is incomplete.

It's why you're still on the planet. Everything you do —
or don't do — is important. Time is an ally when you live
each day with purpose.

Whatever you project you create.

The only thing real is thought. Everything you see around you was first a thought, including yourself. Be careful what you believe in, because this is what you bring into being.

Extend kindness of every kind to every kind.

Let another person out in traffic. Hold the door for someone. Say hello to a neighbor.

You are part of a higher plan.

You have a connection to an infinite source of greatness and love. In times of trial you may feel estranged from this source. However, it is precisely during these times that you can make an even deeper connection.

Leave tomorrow's worries to tomorrow.

Stay present minded. Why live where you cannot be? Try to release your expectations of an outcome.

You are stronger than you know.

Believe that you will prevail in anything that
comes your way. Allow others to help you through
challenging circumstances. Never lose heart,
never give up, and remove the words
"I can't" from your mind.

You are not your past.

To truly go forward, you must face forward.
Yesterday can restrict you if you allow it to. Every one
of your errors of the past can be erased, but you
must initiate the process.

Someone is watching over you.

You may choose to doubt this or not believe it.

But that does not change the fact that you are cared for,

now and always, by advanced spiritual helpers.

This is one of life's premier truths.

Real wealth appears on no ledger.

Money is not a yardstick by which to measure success. What truly enriches your life—love, learning and peace of mind—cannot be bought. A pauper can be wealthier than a millionaire.

Give the gift of peace.

Share the heartfelt words and images of (fear not) with family
and friends. You can purchase additional copies of this remarkable book
online at: ThreeSpiritsPress.com

Or call us toll-free at 866.550.0149.

Inspire others with your story.

If the messages in this book have helped you experience greater
fulfillment in your life, we invite you to share your story with other
readers in future publications.

Please send an email to: mystory@threespiritspress.com

We welcome all comments and suggestions. Send your email to
publisher@threespiritspress.com

Or write to us at:

Three Spirits Press
P.O. Box 832
Welches, Oregon 97067

About the author:

Alan Lohner is a lifelong creative writer who earned a master's degree in journalism from the University of Oregon. He's a native of Toledo, Ohio, where he served as a police officer from 1976 to 1980. He lives in suburban Portland, Oregon with his two sons, Alan Jr. and Joseph, and their two pet dachshunds, Rocky and Howard.

About the photographer:

Jason Savage has an uncanny talent for capturing the offbeat and dramatic behind his photo lens. He is an award-winning photographer who holds a Bachelor of Fine Arts degree from Indiana University. Jason grew up in the Hoosier State and relocated to the Pacific Northwest in 2003.

About the designer:

Cory Raff has more than 20 years of experience in graphic design. He's operated his own advertising and design business since 1985. He's a native of Gresham, Oregon and he earned an associate's degree in design at Mount Hood Community College.

Today is the only day you have.

Smile at a stranger. Forgive your past. Appreciate your life from this moment forward.